Forty Poems
and the Lovers

Forty Poems and the Lovers

Bunches and Smore

SAY SAY

ARCHWAY
PUBLISHING

Archway Publishing books may be ordered through booksellers or by contacting:

Archway Publishing
1663 Liberty Drive
Bloomington, IN 47403
www.archwaypublishing.com
1 (888) 242-5904

ISBN: 978-1-4808-7749-8 (sc)
ISBN: 978-1-4808-7748-1 (e)

Library of Congress Control Number: 2019904844

Print information available on the last page.

Archway Publishing rev. date: 4/23/2019

%@%%^%^%^%^%^%^%A^%^%^%^%^%^%^%^%@%

From; Beguilement at my heels you're a sweet rose
To; To me you sting to hear
From; Does the stinger fall away and leave me at death's door
To; No you rile in the flesh of your victim
From; Wonder my victim pours
To; Then more than you expected
From; I conceal my sting
To; Your pull is felt
From; Do I go for more
To; More again what would that be called
From; Again
To; More
From; Again
To; No more
From; You bow
To; Against myself I am proud
From; I pull you and you still are proud
To; I resist
From; I persist
To; I resist
From; I insist I am together with you pulling you
To; I resist
From; I am at your gates ramming
To; Ram you will not break my stone
From; Ram, I broke your stone
To; My stone is broken
From; Ram I persist
To; My stones are broken
From; Ram I persist
To; My stones are soft and breeze blows away my walls
From; I expose you
To; I am exposed

From; Suppose I have you over yourself
To; I suppose
From; You suppose
To; I suppose
From; I impose
To; I am posed
From; I am in you supposed
To; You suppose me for a fool
From; I have your gates fallen and you posed what more
To; Again
From; What more
To; Again
From; No more just my victory over you
To; I am a hide of marble. Clear to see yet more I conceal than you see
From: I am your steady polish. At your grain in earnest work
To; I shiver for you
From; I am at your glide
To; I shine for you
From; I am at your glide
To; I shine
From; I see myself inside you
To; I shine for you
From; I fall in
To; Love takes you into me
From; I fall in to the endless reaches of your embrace
To; How much do you see polish boy
From; I see more
To; How much is more
From; How much more
To; Resistance is futile
From; I am at your prowess
To; You are bound to my embrace
From; Together endless
To; To tomorrow two tonight

From; Two more spell the night under the stars

To; Two more spell the night for the stars

From; Two more spell the light for the sight

To; Two more the spell is broken

From; Two more the spell is forgotten

To; Two more and the spell is gone

From; Two more fall under the stars

To; Two more fell but there were no stars

From; Two more take the plunge

To; Two more lost under the surf

From; Two more lose their power

To; The tide tells the tale at the beach

From; The beach tells the tale at the grass's edge

To; The grass cannot understand

From; The message in a bottle

To; Is lost

From; What becomes of love when mystery hides the message

To; Love takes every way to the day of resurrection

From; Love is reborn

To; To me I am mother

From; From you I am father

To; From me you are prowler

From; To me you are empowered

To; From me you are endowed

From; By the creator to love's end

To; Love loves the ends

From; The two are love's in and out

To; The two are love's heart and hold

From; The two are love's second breath

To; The two are love is reborn

From; The two are at the grass reborn

To; For what grass could not convey was rebirth

From; For what was love reborn

To; For more was love reborn

From; For what was unfinished at the end
To; For what was finished at the end
From; Forms at the beginning

%@%%^%^%^%^%^%B^%^%^%^%^%^%^%@%

From; From me you won't get far anywhere
To; To me you can't stay far
From; From we what gathers
To; Wait a while and see
From; While I wait which way did the moon break beneath the sea
To; Count your wait and which way was the moon falling
From; While I count which way was the compass bent
To; To the East and broke beneath the sheets of foam
From; My heart
To; My heat
From; How far beneath the sheets
To; Far enough to find the streets
From; How far beneath the sheets
To; Far enough to reach the streaks
From; How far to reach the streaks
To; Far enough to see
From; That which my disdain aches to strain
To; Love that can't be in vain
From; Love that takes the pain
To; I sear in my dropping rate
From; I your spear to the pain
To; I meet pain
From; I before you raise to the fiend
To; Pain
From; I stab
To; Pain again
From; I stab again
To; My mind sits idle

From; I move the spread parting of the flesh in pain
To; The flesh moves
From; Against me
To; The flesh grooves
From; I catch
To; I am caught
From; You are caught with a lashing flutter
To; I am lashed
From; You are caught and lashed
To; I am raised and red
From; Your lashing will not end
To; I am reeling and red at my end
From; Your end will not be yet
To; Who saves me
From; Beneath you your savior comes
To; I am surprised
From; A grip
To; Grip what do you hold
From; All the worlds
To; Count to me how many
From; Six to the stars and twelve to the sands
To; Love at the mind
From; How do I find
To; Look for the tower over the land
From; I am lost
To; Look for the tower take the line
From; I am caught you are the line
To; I am between you
From; I am
To; The tower sheds for you
From; Covering
To; Love to silence a foul
From; Silence the fool
To; Words to aide me

From; Thistles
To; The sting of the silence invited
From; Empty breaths leave silence to the wind
To; Empty has my eyes fixed
From; My quest
To; Fill my empty eyes
From; Request
To; Yours for a chance
From; To take you
To; Empty
From; From empty to plenty
To; Empty at every side to me is too plenty
From; Empty at my side to me you are plenty
To; Find me at the water's merging

%@%%^%^%^%^%^%^%C^%^%^%^%^%^%^%^%@%

Waves render to my sight
Cast visions pulled from the surf
Tender childhood's memories
Pull the air from my lungs
Ripples under the surf
The clouds under the surf
The waves bend away
The bubbles flutter to freedom
My last sight is eternity

%@%%^%^%^%^%^%^%D^%^%^%^%^%^%^%^%@%

I sat in silence with patience
Stones stood to greet the sky
The clouds bellowed
Thunder touched the ground
Cataclysm called from the dark place

The light spear buried the land
The earth was born

%@%%^%^%^%^%^%^%E^%^%^%^%^%^%^%@%

Gliding glittering gleaming sprite.
For a moment with me
For a moment you are my sight
For a moment together
For an eternity apart.

%@%%^%^%^%^%^%^%F^%^%^%^%^%^%^%@%

Two with love on the breeze
The lead to dip the tail to follow
The wind to catch
The passion to hold
The waves to wonder
The earth to part
The moment to the wind
Love last to the break of the clouds
Resurrects and glides away

%@%%^%^%^%^%^%^%G^%^%^%^%^%^%^%@%

Withering winds calling from high
Where does the sky stop
Withering height spanning farther than the sky
Where does infinity fade
Eternal darkness our overlord
where does the human mind get that from
God
where did the light go
Glory

When does the light go away
Death
I wait
Dementor
Even though my form has given
Wrought
Even before my decent into the grave
Diaspora
Even with one form
What spans my conscious across the cosmic abyss
God
God I have given my last
Salvation
A sinner's delight
Mercy
Make a return after the return and more
Depth
Suffocate my emptiness
Breath
Stop a while and rest
Sleep
When will I have time to speak
Express
What a joke
Expression
What does the concept assume
No bias
What does the concept express
Bias.

%@%%^%^%^%^%^%^%H^%^%^%^%^%^%^%^%@%

Lasting hours of the night
The gathering of hollow spirits

Friends have gathered to me
Speak the day's folly and fiddle me to the roof

Lasting hours of the night
The gathering of the horrified spirits
Fortunate to gather to me
Speak the day's tragedy and find me on the roof

Lasting hours of the night
The gathering of the sold spirits
Fortune gathers you to me
Speak the day's commands or fall from the roof

The last hours of the time of prophecy
The window to the other world closes
Good bye hollows
Good bye horror
Good bye sold

%@%%^%^%^%^%^%^%I^%^%^%^%^%^%^%^%^%@%

Fair does the flower smell
Far about does the flower fill
With lavender and rose
Tulip and daffodil
Sweet marigold and buttercup pinch
For tender persuasion
of any with scent to smell her

%@%%^%^%^%^%^%^%J^%^%^%^%^%^%^%^%^%@%

Fire flowers burns at the field of battle
The dead and the dying lie in amber embrace
The fallen and the fierce follow each other

As the scent and the smell trail the wind
The clash of swords sends through the breeze
The flare of blood baths the prairie in blood's red
As lilacs lie in wait for that day of wonder and magic
Hands fly and swords fly and hilts fly and hands fly
As roses gem anew under the undisturbed soils
Chains of armor and chains of arms and chains capture the weak
Four rose bushes meet a flame
Three sages and two priests still in prayer at the top of the steps
War needs no prophets only prospects
Blood of the wise seep down the walls of the alter
Still and silence take their bows
Surrender leaves nothing to remember
War needs no prisoners
Two years and the village is renewed in fire flowers

%@%%^%^%^%^%^%K^%^%^%^%^%^%^%@%

Wither wonders which way does the golden fox play
Wither beneath my empty feet what has the breeze brought
Cold in spells and cold in wells and ice to the touch
The cold claims the season for a hold

Wither and wonder as the golden fox plays
Take the eve of spring and return to your snowed in den
Leave a trail and chase your tail and find the cold gives way
Play a day and play away the cold beneath your den

Golden fox pray tell do the seasons change your color
Golden fox swim well lead a waking rise for the other
Golden fox prey there lead a silent waltz to the other
Amber fox to the other sniffles my belly is dry

Merriment and there she went the pups to feed a sunder
Curls and twirls and mothers eyes to see the two over and under
Rumbles and tussles to witness the pups
Cuffs and paws to the chin

%@%%^%^^%^%^%^%^%L^%^%^%^%^%^%^%^%@%

When in the last night
The dying King
Spoke to the lord
Seven sons about
He spoke this kind

When in the Red Sea
The born and yet to be
King of the Israel
Spoke to the lord
He spoke this kind

When in the Isle of man
Treachery took the mind of man
Misery mistook the land as fine
Bitterly he shook and spoke this kind
When in the last night he spoke

Pharos bound about
The bondage of his kind
The ailing of them like kine
The wailing of weak rang
Through the minds
When in the last night
The dying King spoke

He who set me upon Israel
Swept me free from obscenity
Sold me satin and palm
Sat with me smoldering and sighed
Smelled at me sweetly and replied
Was that my lord

When in the last night
The dying King spoke
Heaven breathed to behold
The lattice in dying holds
The King spoke this kind

From me did he have my home
From my home did he have my hold
From my hold did he have my bread
From my bread did he have me
From me did he have my worship

When in the last night
The dying king spoke
The lord his only witness
Seven sons shed tears and witness
The King of Israel spoke this kind

%@%%^%^%^%^%^%^%M^%^%^%^%^%^%^%^%@%

I miss
The dream
The time
The place left
The shelter of your arms

I miss
The pace
The everlasting
The grace
The beneficence
The guidance
The embrace

I miss
All the mornings
I miss
Yes I stay here morning
I miss
My Heavenly Father
I miss my Heavenly Father
I miss the days
How an infinite passed in just a spade
I miss my Heavenly Father
Do you miss me father
What will my future hold
Where will my release be
Where will you next meet me
I miss you father because you the source of my soul you are the light
and the hand that casts play
I miss you father come back home
I miss you father please when you have settled
come back or take me with you or get these jerks off my back
Pricy for privacy
The price of privacy is a price no prior would pay I am thankful to have
surrendered my privacy for you father.

%@%%^%^%^%^%^%^%N^%^%^%^%^%^%^%^%@%

At the midnight hour
Set all out with a flower
Set down every tower
Wipe away every hour
At the midnight hour

Time ends
The humans project
A failed collapse
Reset the clock
Start a new
The next breed to the stage
The hour is zero
At the midnight hour
Chuf chuf chuf chuf

At the midnight hour
What was collected
What was affected
What was survived
What was extinguished
Where was the land
Set ablaze
Where the end
Met the end
"Tis 'tis 'tis 'tis

At the midnight hour
Clamber on and returned
To power
Shadows burned and returned
To power
Catchers caught and returned
The fire

Life the gift
To death returned
Tic tic tic tic

At the midnight hour
Water to wine
Dust falls over garden vines
Ashes too hot
Fallout
Fall of the earth
Autumn the last
Winter a tomb
For none to see
For none to be
Breakout
Life the gift
Gone the giver

%@%%^%^%^%^%^%@O^%^%^%^%^%^%^%^%@%

I met a white father
Over his feet
Rising for another
Slow days
The farms in a haze
Small pups at his feet

I met a white mother
Prairie flowers
New phone towers
Dressed Sunday best
No child in distress
Her feet up in rest

I met a white father
Fallen under
Slow days
The farm has been razed
Dust bowl
His progeny will be without
To the trail of labor

I met a white mother
Five under her
Two ill
Eating pennies
Soil over their skin
Toiled over and turned to sin

I met a white father
Sorrow asunder
His flock ill
His wage his own making
Bad farming no taking
Bank loan no pay
All to the reaper
His work gone

%@%%^%^%^%^%^%^%P^%^%^%^%^%^%^%^%@%

I met the end
Over the falls
Catching witness
Pulling, drawing,
Sinking stones
Breaking falls
Take their homage
Naked forms

For the witness
Sin aserts
T'will all be mine

I met the day
Over the moon
Taking witness
Sinking tides
Raising spires
Breaching rocks
Breaking tides
Breathing winds
Captured stone
Forms to man
He sits inspired

I met epiphany
To her the swells
To change the hearts
To take the mind
To see in stars
The name of witness

I met glory
Over the end
Singing stories
From the end
Meeting me
Leading me
Treating me
As only me

%@%%^%^%^%^%^%^%Q^%^%^%^%^%^%^%^%@%

I met a black father
Two daughters
Three in the water
Settled waves
Small hands
Slow days
Father's gaze
Healing

I met a black father
Prairie light
Cannon foder
Seven after his feet
Eight hundred for him complete
Running through the meadow
Bumped and bruised
Free man lives today

I met a black mother
Low down asking for another
Holy hands
Burned feet
Three seventy keep the kids
Free woman
Born under his feet

I met a black mother
Two to her waist
Each another's
Reaches
Over her head
What she cannot reach
Her own head

I met a black man
Fallen
Low down asking and calling
Broke down
Stealing and brawling
His end had no witness

I met a black woman
Searching
Low down basking and thawing
All the days at her asking and gnawing
She waits for a savior
Her end has no patron sent

%@%%^%^%^%^%^%R^%^%^%^%^%^%^%@%

Floor bartered baked and rye
Swells and smells with cakes and wines
Send me the fork and part me with wine
Reach me with rye parched and dry
Scatter the sugar and taste the sweat
Pain lingers over the bee stings
For the taste of her nectar
Let the sting linger more
What Gamora and Chang
Romeo and Juliet
The lovers and the heart
Did not part with was
The catcher and the rye
Long I take my trying tastes
Hard I endure my testimony
That to rye I deliver my brooding
She bakes for my eye
That someday she parts cakes

Over my eyes
Longer I linger
For the day I part her and see
What span she reaches
What depth she knows
What rhetoric she persuades
What calm she exudes
The rye bakes to the heat
Flesh aches to the beat
For someday many
Upon her drums I beat
The deep beat

%@%%^%^%^%^%^%^%S^%^%^%^%^%^%^%^%@%

My heart is a miss
For my glory sits away from me
Seven lands and I have not seen
Her sight and her serenity

My heart is a miss
For her heat is not mine
All of mine

Where have the days gone
When love leapt into my eyes
Where do the embers go
When fire breathes alone

Where does she sit away from me
For to find her I would give my crime
I creed and I cry and I live and I die
But Loni with your love I will not alone

For to hold your heat upon my flesh
Smother myself between your love
Scares would the guise see us

%@%%^%^%^%^%^%T^%^%^%^%^%^%^%@%

Satin folds curls
Steady underneath
Hearts abound
To see what lies
Beneath
Vestige of alms
Coy invested arms
My tickles your tithing
Giggles underwhelm
By closed lips
By shared hips
By the day we break
By the night we make
Morning baked
Noon from me takes
Sunset never seen
Dark colored steam
To the moon we disembark
To each and in the other
We mark
Love to the love at love
Find me again

%@%%^%^%^%^%^%U^%^%^%^%^%^%^%@%

White mother white child
White car wide smile

Are you going to text your phone
No I will stress you and hope to atone

White mother white child
Mother's trial to pull back but go forward
Child's idols move under her eyes
Are you going
Only if he lets me

White mother white child
How long has been your trial
Journey on reverse
Pull back
The curb is under you

%@%%^%^%^%^%^%^%V^%^%^%^%^%^%^%^%@%

White mother wild child
Small car late style
Are you the dream unbound
Does the sting set off chains
Does opium know you by name

White mother wonder child
Class kept but no lessons learned
Child taught to walk, talk, and stand proud
Sits steady freeway outbound

White mother stiff hold
Breath more, steady loose control
Over the limit under exposed
Find a medic recover from the brink
Stings of her father
Only if he didn't let you

White mother wild child
How long has been your trial
Journey on change
Pull back
Don't blow the vein
Life spent all in vain

%@%%^%^%^%^%^%^%W^%^%^%^%^%^%^%^%@%

Black mother black child
Black lick no smiles
Are you going to text your phone
Only if my phone will atone to the satellites

Black mother black child
Black berry raw child
Mother's trials to put back to go free
Child's idols wear crosses under their eyes
Are you going
Only if he lets me

Black mother black child
Hear the harping cry coming from afar
How long did mother bleed
How many faces did you see
Mother's heart rests over her soul
Black child you go on your own.

%@%%^%^%^%^%^%^%X^%^%^%^%^%^%^%^%@%

Black mother stone child
Strong grip no smile
Are you gonna text back
Study time can't wait

Black mother solo time
My ambitions my time
Are you gonna study all night
Steady yourself I'm on the rise

Black mother strong child
Can't miss if I don't slide
Long nights no help
Child's idols were born to different times

Black mother college woman
Find the man that knows he's the one
Find the stone that steadies into one
Black value slim pickings
Cotton days cloudy haze
Black man's turn to rise

%@%%^%^%^%^%^%^%Y^%^%^%^%^%^%^%^%@%

Four moons over foreign worlds
The rising spires of fallen worlds
Haunted hills of bitter wreckage
Skies of deep and omnipotent ruin
The winds of oblivion have entered
The soiled soils of superior set to fire
The rivers leave the land in scars
The stellar glows to the fallen
Life left ominous in stones grip
What names lie beneath the ember glow
Fire the last to die against the setting suns

%@%%^%^%^%^%^%^%Z^%^%^%^%^%^%^%^%@%

Snow by the water over the sea
Pray tell what comes in threes
My journey forbids
Rain to the leaf folding heavy
Pray tell what falls and frees
My joining commits
Star light to the dark embrace
Pray tell what streaks we seek
My journey forbids
Landing fowl over the lake
Pray tell what catches you beneath
My joining commits
Fish free beneath the sea
Pray tell what finds the leak
My journey forbids
Sea the stars to bid farewell

%@%%^%^%^%^%^%^%A^%^%^%^%^%^%^%^%@%

I solemn words do say
Seldom will once be exchanged
I breach from far and yonder deep
Found my journey the hearts to keep
I calling of the wind breath from afar
Greetings to meet you and greet you
I wild spirit sailing between wind and water
Frolic about your company
I tree sprout to you stand to you
To gather with you the fruits of my labor
I sweet rose fold in waiting for your eyes
Come from far and part me with a fingertip
I blossom true and flawless find me already parted for your eyes
I lilac in winter or in spring will wait to with you sing
I lotus over the water meet you with a gift

I blossom return with twice my earning to reap
I Jade sit deep with the crown in waiting
I crescent moon over your eyes look down and grin
I tide with the moon meet you with humble grin
I sapphire stone sit on earnest throne
I sapphire with life breeze about
I sparrow at the wind
I hawk sail
I dove at your feet
I smaller and flee to meet
I bark
I follow the bark and keen are my feet
I frolic with hop and bound
Two ears erect and nose around
I wild hog
I slither beneath your senses
I still and stiff to move watch my eyes
I a wasp sting thy eyes
I bumble at the grin and meet the Lilly lilac and blossom
I hold all to the end

%@%%^%^%^%^%^%^%B^%^%^%^%^%^%^%^%@%

Tender flower's child
What moves your fragile eyes
Tender flower's child
How now you've grown proud
Tender flower's child
Hop and bound hope is in bound
Tender flower's child
Wonder what makes your eyes shake
Tender flower's child
Mother's might is yours for delight
Tender flower's child

Follow eager and follow close
Mother's might is your old post
Tender flower's child
Lips squeeze on dumplings pleased
Tender flower's child
Shine and shiver your eyes are rivers
Swim and spin spear fish and sing
Tender flower's child
Call to the wind with raspberry grin
Grandmother's boasting brother's win
Tender flower's child
Run fast and lean against the edge
Run now and learn again the end

%@%%^%^%^%^%^%^%C^%^%^%^%^%^%^%^%@%

Little lilac to the embers falling
Do you come to wake me for spring
Little daisy from afar to the rising heat
Do you come to wake me for spring
Little damsels to the bowing smolder
Do you come to wake me for spring
Little tulips gathered near a kindle to the blowing sky
Do you come to wake me for spring
Little fire fly out by the river's stream
Do you come to wake me for spring
Little lamb out without bounds to the night's red storm
Do you come to wake me for spring
Small foul and fleeing pups
Fire wakes none for spring has come to ruin

%@%%^%^%^%^%^%^%D^%^%^%^%^%^%^%^%@%

Death hosted a deaf man
Who died to the tune of a falling wail
The wind about him told of him well
Death hosted a river stream
Died to the seasons ail and the sun's eye
The wind the keeper of the fallen stream
Death hosted a carting beggar
Who died to the company of virus
The wind still appeared moving farewell
Death hosted a still born infant
Who died before meeting the world
The wind was the first and last touch
Death hosted the king of kings
Stunned silent and sulking
The wind about him inconsolable
Who died was everything
What died was a dream
Death hosted a prairie shrew
Small pickings for the hawk
Who met the end to the beggars way
The wind about the shrew shed away to the stars
Death hosted a spinning fire
Ruin and ruin was left to the wind
Rain

%@%%^%^%^%^%^%^%E^%^%^%^%^%^%^%^%@%

The last hand to the gentle monk
Was over his chest crossed in embrace
As snow fell and the tiger sang
The last to land the first to melt
The monk in silence the tiger sang
The two apart to meet together at the end
The tiger sang and the monk stared

Twilight dawned and the red amber glared
The sun to the west the tiger the sands to the east
Darkness fell as the tiger sang
Together at the end
The cub and the caretaker

%@%%^%^%^%^%^%^%F^%^%^%^%^%^%^%^%@%

High chair fragile infant there
Wonder touch cold ice cream there
Steady arms mother's eyes there
High chair tongue out with a stare
Spoon wide smile tender there
Wide try small returns there
High chair fragile infant stare
Small hands pink blossom rare
Small hands ice cream for mustache
Wave new care slide young hair
Mother's arms the best for care
Follow left follow right
Your nose was captured tight
Follow left follow right
A captured phone yours for the ride
Follow left follow right
Your packed on the baby cart
High chair good bye there
Tomorrow to you comes rare

%@%%^%^%^%^%^%^%G^%^%^%^%^%^%^%^%@%

Brown don't frown
Green share the crown
Love is enough for two blue
Amber mix with the play

Gray try and don't stay away
Some time today pink
Try hard and think silver and pink
Rocky tan try not to grin at your twin
Teal the game is not real play tender
Not the time yellow pretender
Black to the back with you
Follow suit white
Share the edge and pledge
Lime greet your elder
Father time will not long be with us

%@%%^%^%^%^%^%^%H^%^%^%^%^%^%^%^%@%

Coy whispers swimming stars
Thrones of mirrors shimmer by
Cold rises from the stars and
Old currents and young play
Whisper by and head out
To the next day
The water pulls close to play
Whisper's swim together
And closes in to late
Caught two late to swim away
Mirrored in many tails
Dearly beloved beneath the pile
Gathered fish out of water
Tears the whispers unheard by the ears

%@%%^%^%^%^%^%^%H^%^%^%^%^%^%^%^%@%

Ding Ding Dong
The sounds of dying coming over the crown
Death was with me for a while and spoke a while

Does the seat rest against you or the other true
Death I am not candid towards you
Do you know my affections
Death I am not candid towards you
Does the taste of the lamb not grant you salivation
Death I am not candid towards you
Does the taste of victory not give you rise
Death I am not candid
Does the taste of fear not meet you well and clear
No
Does the fear of death not give your life clear life
No
Do you resist life or death
What brings the two together
You do
Death I am not candid towards you
Do you live or do you die
Live
Can any one live or does everyone die
The answer is the truth
The answer is my truth
Death I am not candid towards you
Then be candid towards the standing truth
No
That you are heading towards me and not the other truth
Death I am not candid towards you
Does candid ever get to the end of life
No
Then here's the happy ending

%@%%^%^%^%^%^%^%H^%^%^%^%^%^%^%^%@%

When love found the moon
Did the two embrace the tides

When the oceans crest
Do the fish see the stars
When blood runs over the water
Did the donor meet the end
When love found the moon
Did the mood change
When ocean waves fall
Do they ever reach the bottom
When blood boils
Do we die a little
When love found the moon
Who spoke first
When the tide recedes
What's left on the beach
When blood pools
Where do the flowers go
When love found the moon
Was she dressed
Did the ocean give birth to the wind
Do the stars see our days
Did blood rule over water
When love found the moon
Which sent fire and
Which was white
What does a wave look at for peace
What breaks beneath my feet
Blood seeping slips away the bind
What takes me to mine my mind
What times time's tics
What rhyme is everything
Why did the lovers forget
When love found the moon
Was her father agreed
What broke the peace

When far and freedom fell
What broke the peace
When dire and angels fell
What broke the reach
What spell bond love fled
What morning was bled
When love found the moon
Was it high tide or afternoon
When holy eyes were full
What was beauty behind
When the darling was you
What flower did you send

%@%%^%^%^%^%^%^%I^%^%^%^%^%^%^%^%@%

Death meet me on a spry winter's day
Bring me mother's kiss and the tumor I missed
Take me two days from three
Leave me in the company of none
Set me before the dying sun
Roll me to the sea
When you return count the three
To me let there be no memory
Etch me back into stone
Store my bones for the toll
Leave my flesh for the wanted
Haunt my heart to the last breath
My lungs to the first wreath
Lay my God to the last seat
I will breath again

%@%%^%^%^%^%^%^%J^%^%^%^%^%^%^%^%@%

Falling
Falling
Falling
Far behind
The child of ember cries

Dripping
Flies about
Dripping
Upon high
The child of ember cries

Dreaming
Dark in the night
Dreaming
For morning
The child of ember cries

Drenched
Dreary and
Drenched
Under the skies
The child of ember cries

Solitary
Still and
Solitary
Stricken apart
The child of ember cries

Sagamora
Stoa and
Sutatia

Solutes to the saints
The child of ember cries

%@%%^%^%^%^%^%^%K^%^%^%^%^%^%^%^%@%

Bent little eyes
Far casted
By father's casket
Bent little eyes
What has father
Yet doesn't gather farther
Bent little eyes
What has a sweet melody
Spoken to a closing tune
Bent little eyes
What sees you suffer
Speaks at you through
Bent little eyes
What has brought
Your beginning to this end
Bent little eyes
What is responsible for you
That is not responsive
Bent little eyes
Tantrum bound
Gather with mother
Gather with your soul
Alone is all you own

%@%%^%^%^%^%^%^%L^%^%^%^%^%^%^%^%@%

Horrors and hauntings
Hold meetings for my soul
To capture what in me boasts

To conjure what in flesh bursts
To stifle what in host proclaims
Horrors and hauntings
Hold meetings for my soul
To blight the light that in me knows
To resist the hauntings that with me goes
To insist that little me surely holds
The secret to life and a hidden one too
For what all the sepulchers and the seas know
Is that the horrors and hauntings go in vain
For only the young in the brain know glory and the pain
Know life and the rain
Know death and to explain
The path of light strikes everywhere for heading forward

%@%%^%^%^%^%^%^%M^%^%^%^%^%^%^%^%@%

Sly away laid down to slave away
Bent down to make a way
Raised alms to find a way
Gave part to her within
To see just part of him without
Coins and callous intentions
She's left for the night
The next awaits

%@%%^%^%^%^%^%^%N^%^%^%^%^%^%^%^%@%

I fell a sleep watching Tuesday
Woke up three Wednesday
From Thursday
Sat up saw Sunday
Shining bright was last Monday
Angry plight jumped to Good Friday

Stems and berries sprouted June
Dark days slept with December
Dazzling was the ember
Fire took it all down to the ground
Rain came and washed it all down
Now only the river tells the story

%@%%^%^%^%^%^%^%O^%^%^%^%^%^%^%^%@%

Little love over the new foal sound
Sitting tight to her mother's delight
Where does love take you at night
Little love over the new river stern
A pop to catch and a paddle fin away
Where does love take you at night
Little love over a catcher's eyes and her lies
A pop to catch and too proud to weigh
Where does love take you at night
Little love caught to the two in love
Churning to flirt to the flirt flirting
Where does love take you at night
Little love of the two again in love
Words wonder about you
Where does love take you at night
Little love over the new found gift
A rare play to the child's eyes
Where does love take you at night

%@%%^%^%^%^%^%^%P^%^%^%^%^%^%^%^%@%

Penny count and
A sentence for a dime
My dignity for a dollar
Buy me a cheap offer

Sell me from the offer
Find me a fair price
Take me to market
Thrice returned and still sold
For amber or for coal
The going gets to the old
The still breathing weigh in gold
My mother resting always told
The way of the weary is the silent and sold
A bash to me
She learned slow
To beat the sale
The smart sell

%@%%^%^%^%^%^%^%Q^%^%^%^%^%^%^%^%@%

Golden eyes
Leaving lines
Fanning far
Set your stare
Send my eyes far and scare
Fall away from the fruit
Fanning out from the root
Features of ravens wings
Fear in me to repeat
Golden eyes set their
Gaze on mine

%@%%^%^%^%^%^%^%^%^%^%^%^%^%^%@%

Printed in the United States
By Bookmasters